Critical Thinking for Kindergarten and Grade 1

(Supplemental workbook for CogAT®, OLSAT® and NNAT® and GATE® Testing)

Authored by Bright Minds Publishing

Copyright© by Bright Minds Publishing. All the questions have been prepared by staff at Bright Minds Publishing.

CogAT® is a registered trademark of Houghton Mifflin Harcourt™. OLSAT® and NNAT2®/NNAT3® are registered trademarks of Pearson Education™.

Houghton Mifflin Harcourt, Pearson Education was not involved in authoring this book in any way. This is not an official or certified guide to the CogAT, OLSAT and NNAT test.

No part of this book may be distributed, photocopied or edited without written consent from the author.

Bright Minds Publishing

Contents

Match Colors and Shapes 4

Match only Colors 5

Match Shading 6

Number sequence 7

Deducing Numbers 8

Connect Dots to form Shapes 9

Tracing Dots 10

3 Sisters 11

Matching Owls 12

Matching Sizes 13

Matching Pairs 14

Coloring Activity 15

Describing objects 16

Matching Shadows 17

Finding Color Patterns 18

Match Stars 19

Overlapping Shapes 20

Similar ladybugs 21

Shape Sequence 22

Number Sequence (Bouncing Ball) 24

Alphabet Sequence 25

Color Sequence 26

Missing Arrow 27

Tangled Balloons 28

Hidden Numbers 29

Hidden Numbers 30

Grandma's knitting Pattern #1 31

Grandma's knitting Pattern #2 32

Grandma's knitting Pattern #3 33

Find Differences #1 34

Find Differences #2 35

Find Differences #3 36

Find Differences #4 37

Find differences #5 38

Math Match 39

Animals in various shapes 40

Counting shapes #1 41

Counting Shapes #2 42

Triangular Maze 43

Matching art tiles 44

Find hidden Objects #1 45

Find hidden Objects #2 46

Find hidden Objects #3 47

Find hidden Objects #4 48

Find hidden Objects #5 49

Ball and the Box 50

Identifying Objects 51

Puzzling Family 52

Bug Search 53

Block Diagram Cut-out 55

Paper Folding 58

Answer Key 61

Match Colors and Shapes

Match the colors and shapes of objects in Column #1 to the colors and shapes from the Column #2.

Column #1	Column #2
A. (blue square)	1. (orange circle)
B. (yellow oval)	2. (green hexagon)
C. (orange circle)	3. (blue square)
D. (green hexagon)	4. (yellow oval)

Match only Colors

Match only the colors of objects in Column #1 to the colors of objects in column #2.

Column #1	Column #2
A. (blue square)	1. (green circle)
B. (yellow oval)	2. (orange square)
C. (orange circle)	3. (yellow pentagon)
D. (green hexagon)	4. (blue oval)

Match Shading

Match fill patterns for objects in Column #1 to fill pattern for objects from Columns #2

Column #1	Column #2
A. (square with diagonal lines)	1. (hexagon with grid pattern)
B. (oval with woven/basket pattern)	2. (triangle with diagonal lines)
C. (hexagon with grid pattern)	3. (square with woven/basket pattern)
D. (triangle with woven/basket pattern)	4. (oval with woven/basket pattern)

Page 5

Number sequence

Complete the number sequence below by finding what number goes in place of the Question Mark (?)

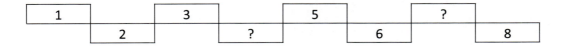

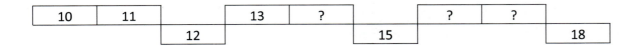

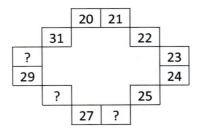

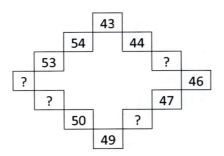

Deducing Numbers

Based on the following clues deduce and guess the number.

Clue #1: The number is between 1 and 10
Clue #2: The number is greater than 5
Clue #3: The number is greater than 7
Clue #4: The number is less than 9

What is the number?

===

Clue #1: The number is a 2 digit number
Clue #2: When you subtract 2 from this number, you get a one digit number
Clue #3: The number is greater than 10

What is the number?

===

Clue #1: The number is between 1 and 20
Clue #2: The digit in the units place is 5
Clue #3: The number is greater than 10

What is the number?

===

Clue #1: The number is between 11 and 15
Clue #2: The number is an even number
Clue #3: The number is closer to 15 than to 11

What is the number?

Connect Dots to form Shapes

For each of the shapes below, start at 1 and connect the dots to form shapes.

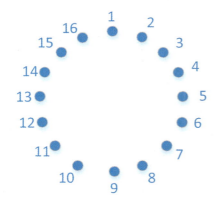
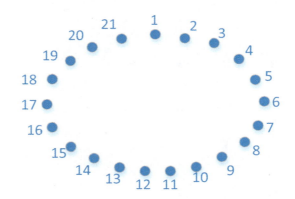
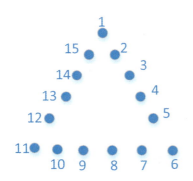
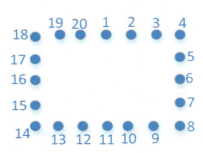
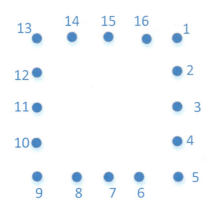
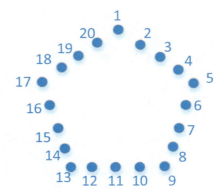

Tracing Dots

Trace the patterns on the left into the grid on the right side

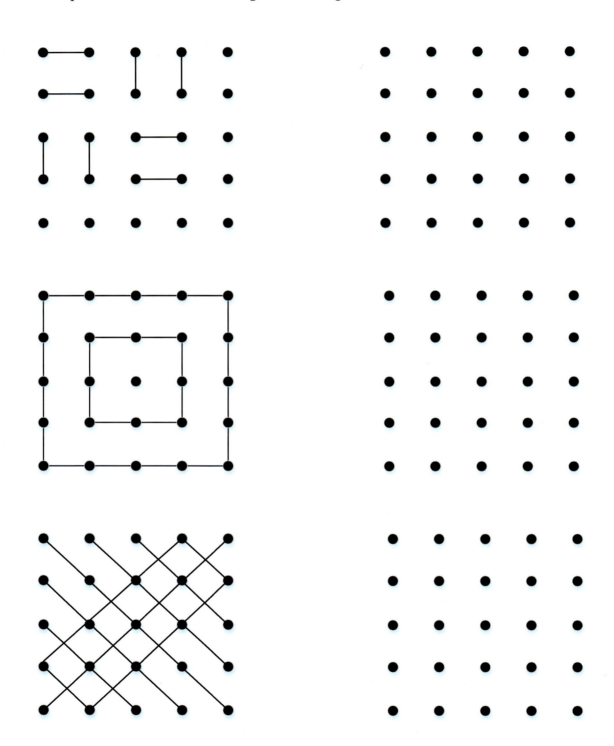

Page 9

3 Sisters

Anna, Beth and Celeste are 3 sisters. With the following clues, can you guess who is the youngest one and the oldest of the 3 sisters?

Clue #1: Anna is not the youngest one.
Clue #2: Beth is not the oldest one.
Clue #3: Celeste is neither the oldest nor the youngest one.

===

Anna, Beth and Celeste are into either water polo, biking or rugby. With the following clues, can you guess who plays what sport?

Clue #1: Anna doesn't like water sports.
Clue #2: Beth doesn't like biking cross country.
Clue #3: Celeste loves to play Rugby.

===

Anna, Beth and Celeste liked different cuisines. With the following clues, can you guess their favorite cuisine

Clue #1: Anna loves Italian Food
Clue #2: Beth doesn't like Greek Food but loves French Food
Clue #3: Celeste is opposite of Beth in terms of her favorite food.

Matching Owls

Draw a line between 2 Owls that have the same shape and color.

Page 11

Matching Sizes

Match the size of objects in Column #1 to the size of objects in column #2.

Column #1	Column #2
A.	1.
B.	2.
C.	3.
D.	4.

Matching Pairs

Match the pair of shapes in Column #1 to the pair of shapes from column #2.

Column #1	Column #2
A.	1.
B.	2.
C.	3.
D.	4.

Page 13

Coloring Activity

Use crayons or colored pencils to color the pattern below to look just like the pattern on the top.

Describing objects

Match the description of objects in Column #1 to the objects in Column #2

Column #1	Column #2
A. Red triangle inside a yellow circle	1.
B. Blue square inside red rectangle	2.
C. Yellow circle inside red triangle	3.
D. Blue triangle inside green pentagon	4.
E. Yellow square inside green circle	5.

Matching Shadows

Draw a line between each animal and its shadow.

Finding Color Patterns

Find the Patterns #1, #2, #3 and #4 in the Main pattern

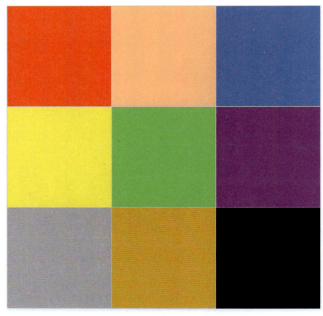

Main Pattern

#1

#2

#3

#4

Match Stars

Match the shapes of stars in column #1 with shape of stars in column #2

Column #1   Column #2

Overlapping Shapes

Study the diagram below and answer questions about how various shapes overlap.

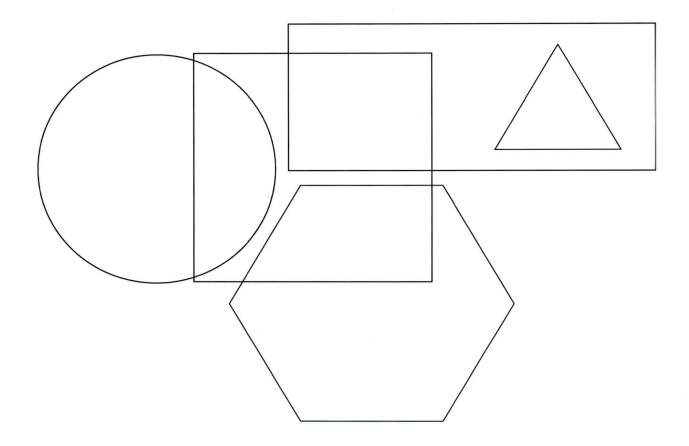

Does the Circle overlap with the Square?	Yes or No
Does the Square overlap with the Rectangle?	Yes or No
Does the Rectangle overlap with the Circle?	Yes or No
Does the Hexagon overlap with the Triangle?	Yes or No
Does the Circle overlap with the Triangle?	Yes or No
Does the Hexagon overlap with the circle	Yes or No

Similar ladybugs

Only two of the ladybugs below are similar can you spot which 2 are similar to each other?

Shape Sequence

Circle the shape that should come next in the sequence of shapes given.

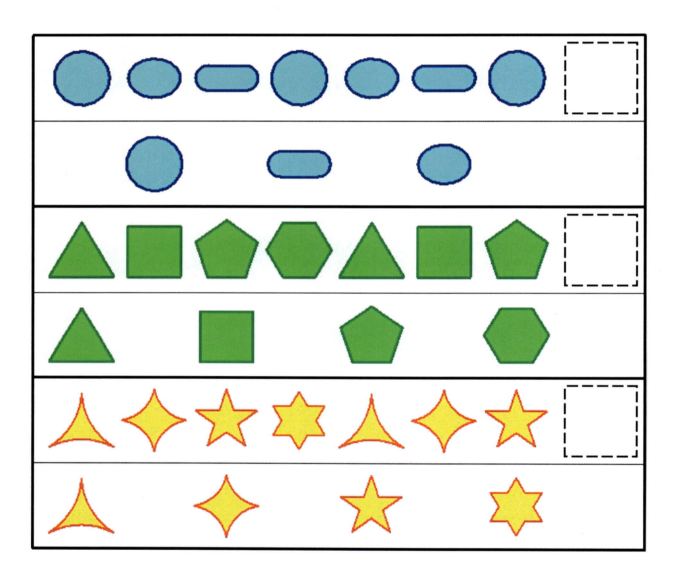

Number Sequence (Leaping Frog)

Where would the leaping frog land next?

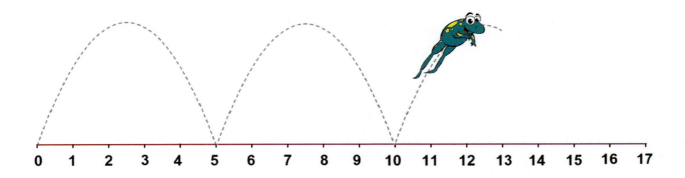

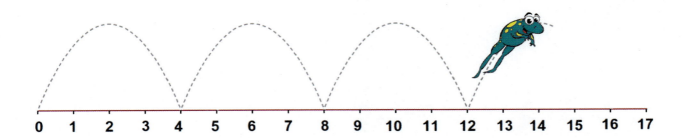

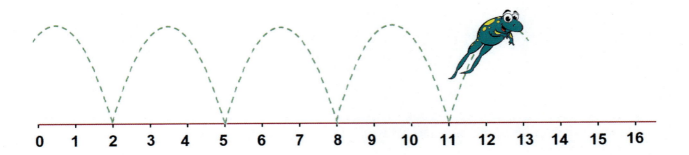

Number Sequence (Bouncing Ball)

Where would the ball land next?

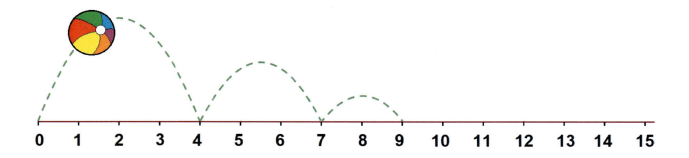

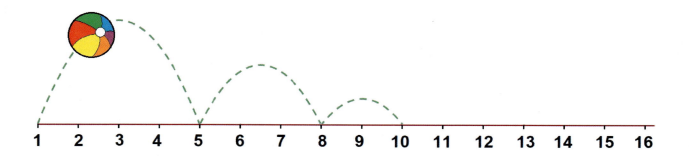

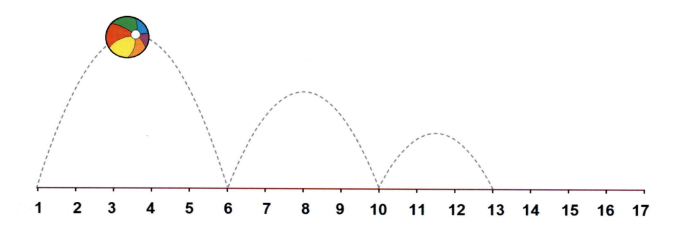

Alphabet Sequence

Which alphabet would come next in the sequence?

A B C A B C A _

B B Q B B Q B B Q _

P Q R S P Q R S P _

X Y Z Z X Y Z Z X _

Color Sequence

Which color would come next in the sequence?

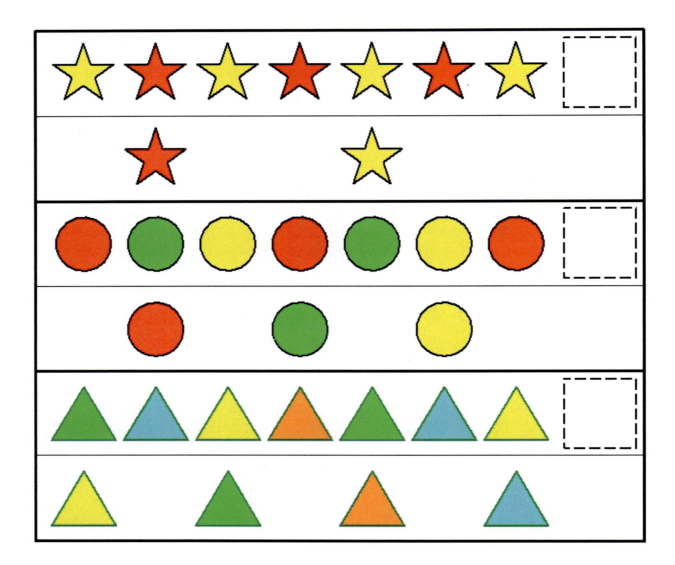

Page 25

Missing Arrow

Box #1 and Box #2 both have various types of arrows. Find which arrow is present in Box #1 and missing from Box #2

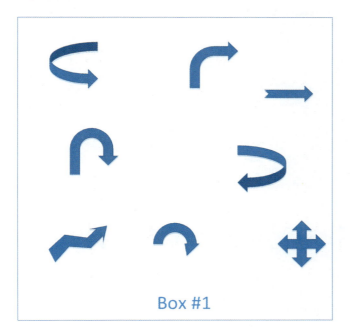

Box #1

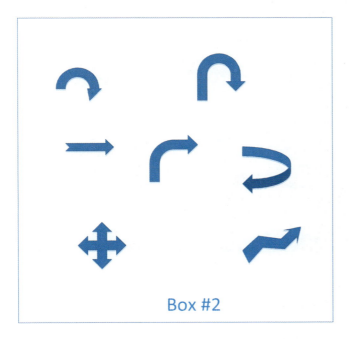

Box #2

Tangled Balloons

Martin, Mary, John and Ashley went to the county fair and bought balloons. Their balloons got tangled. Can you find who bought which balloon?

Hidden Numbers

In the mosaic design below there are numbers that are hidden. Can you find the numbers and color them?

Hidden Numbers

In the mosaic design below there are numbers that are hidden. Can you find the numbers and color them?

Grandma's knitting Pattern #1

See the patterns on the top row and color the other rows.

Grandma's knitting Pattern #2

See the patterns on the top row and color the row below.

Grandma's knitting Pattern #3

See the patterns on the top row and color the row below.

Find Differences #1

Find the difference between the two pictures below

Find Differences #2

Find the differences between the two images.

Find Differences #3

Find the differences between the two images.

Page 35

Find Differences #4

Find the differences between the two images.

Find differences #5

Find the differences between the two images.

Math Match

Match the pair of numbers with the same result

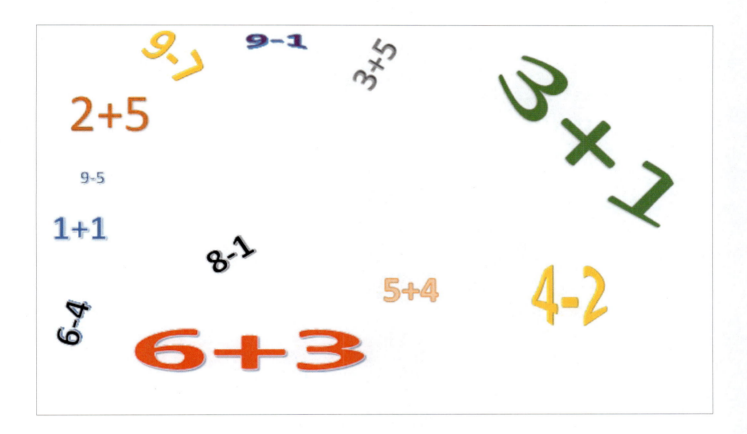

Animals in various shapes

Study the shapes and the position of the animals below. Answer questions below about how the animals are placed in the diagram

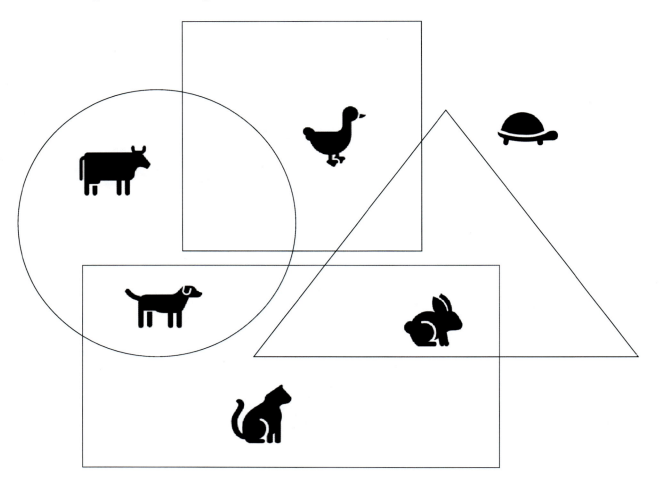

Which animal is inside the square?
Which animal is inside the circle as well as the rectangle?
Which animal or animals are inside the circle?
Which animal or animals are inside the rectangle?
Which animal or animals are not inside any of the shapes?

Counting shapes #1

Count the various shapes in the figure below

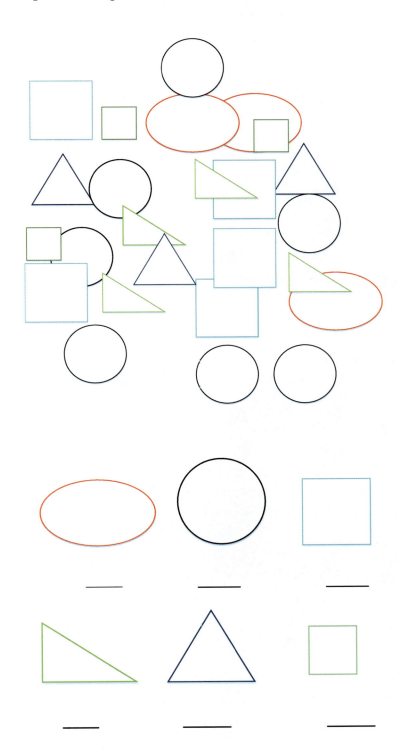

Counting Shapes #2

Count the various shapes in each figure

Triangular Maze

Show the spaceship the path to the center of this triangular maze?

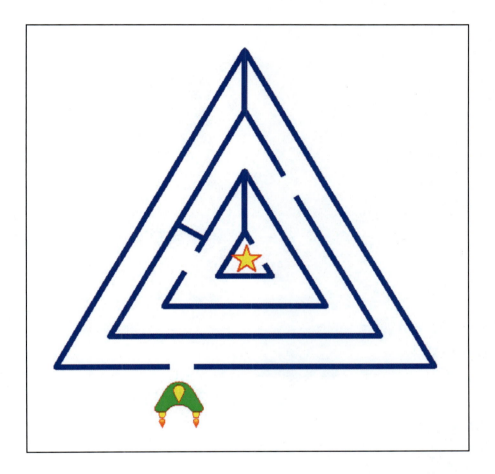

Matching art tiles

Draw a line between matching art tiles

Find hidden Objects #1

Find the objects from the top row in the picture below.

Find hidden Objects #2

Find the objects from the top row in the picture below.

Find hidden Objects #3

Find the objects from the top row in the picture below.

Find hidden Objects #4

Find the objects from the top row in the picture below.

Find hidden Objects #5

Find the objects from the top row in the picture below.

Ball and the Box

Select the word/words that describes the position of the ball

The ball is (**in front of** / **behind**) the box	The ball is (**in front of** / **behind**) the box
The ball is (**inside** / **outside**) the box	The ball is (**inside** / **outside**) the box
The ball is (**on** / **under**) the box	The ball is (**on** / **under**) the box
The ball is (**above** / **below**) the box	The ball is (**above** / **below**) the box
The ball is on (**left** / **right**) of the box	The ball is on (**left** / **right**) of the box

Identifying Objects

1. Which of the following would you wear to protect your head from the cold?

    A   B   C   D

2. Which of the following would you use to protect your eyes from the sunlight?

    A   B   C   D

3. Which of the following has a hard and thorny skin?

    A   B   C   D

Puzzling Family

1. Jessica Johnson has a younger brother Alex Johnson. Alex is taller than Jessica. Jessica's mother Alicia is taller than Alex. Which picture below would be the right picture for the family?

    A   **B**   **C**   **D**

2. Victoria got into trouble and was given a timeout and asked to spend the day in her room. She was not allowed to play with her video games or dolls or watch TV. Which is the one object she can use in her room during her timeout?

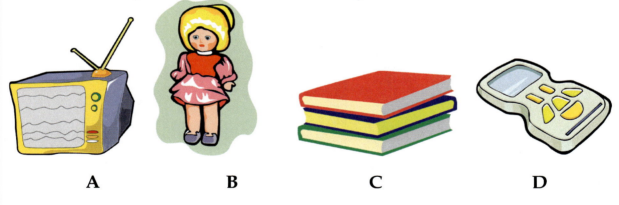

    A   **B**   **C**   **D**

3. Mary's younger brother is 5 years old. Her older brother is 9 years old. How old can Mary be?

5   9   7   11

    A   **B**   **C**   **D**

Bug Search

1. See the picture of the bug inside the box. Search for the same bug in the group of bugs marked #1 to #5.

       #1   #2   #3   #4   #5

2. See the picture of the bug inside the box. Search for the same bug in the group of bugs marked #1 to #5.

       #1   #2   #3   #4   #5

3. See the picture of the bug inside the box. Search for the same bug in the group of bugs marked #1 to #5.

       #1   #2   #3   #4   #5

This page left blank intentionally

Block Diagram Cut-out

Instructions:

Use your parents help to cut out these shapes below. See the problems in this section and try to construct them using the shapes that you cut out.

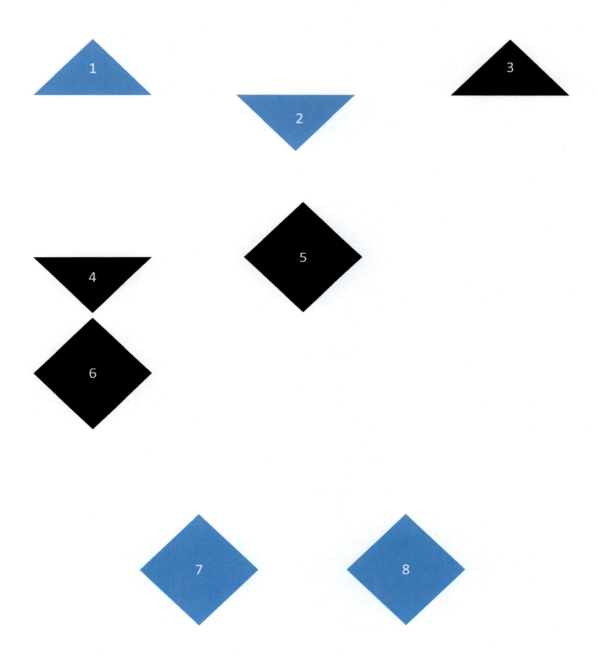

This page left blank intentionally

1. Using the cut-out pieces, construct the following diagram

2. Using the cut-out pieces, construct the following diagram

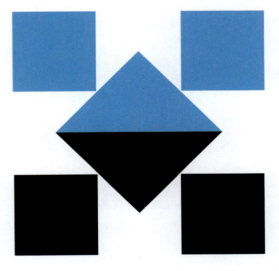

3. Using the cut-out pieces, construct the following diagram.

4. Using the cut-out pieces, construct the following diagram.

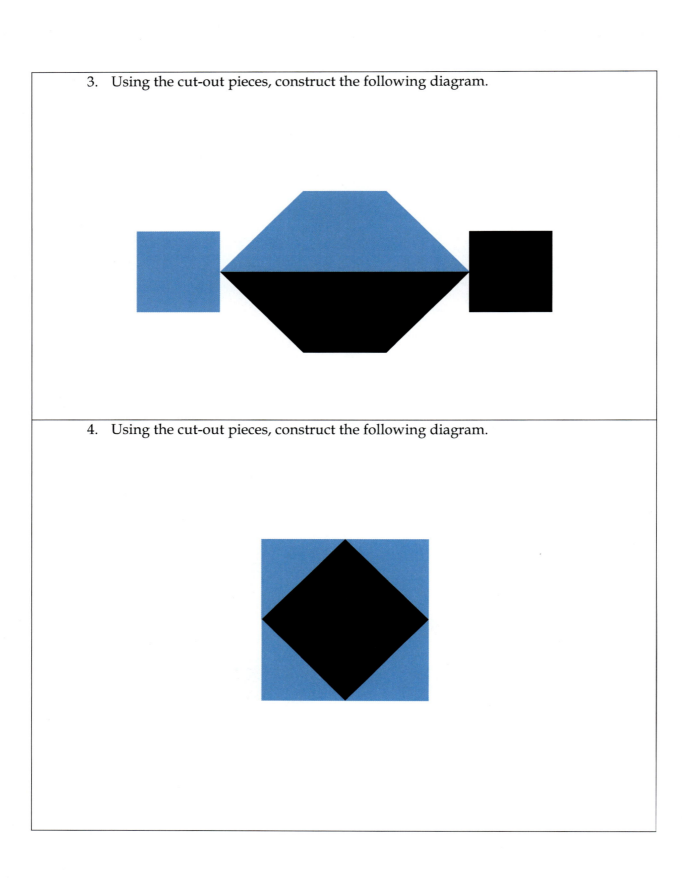

Page 57

Paper Folding

Instructions:

Here is a sample question in this section:

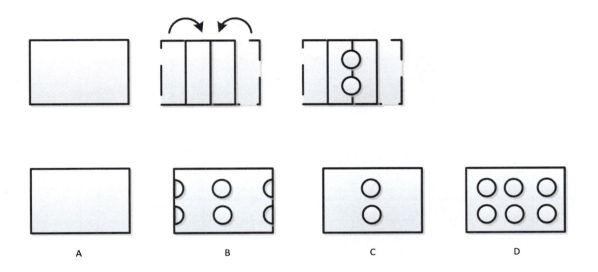

In each question, you are shown a piece of paper that is being folded. Then a hole is punched in the folded piece of paper. Visualize what the paper will look like when it is unfolded. Now look at the answer choices. The unfolded paper should like one of the answer choices.

Here option B is the answer. When you open up the folds, the paper will look like option B.

All the questions in this section can be solved in the same manner.

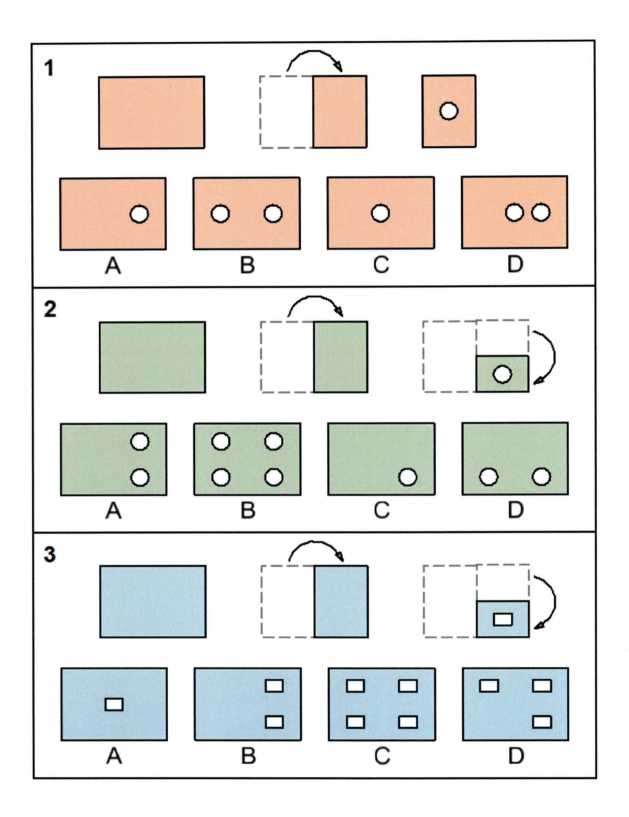

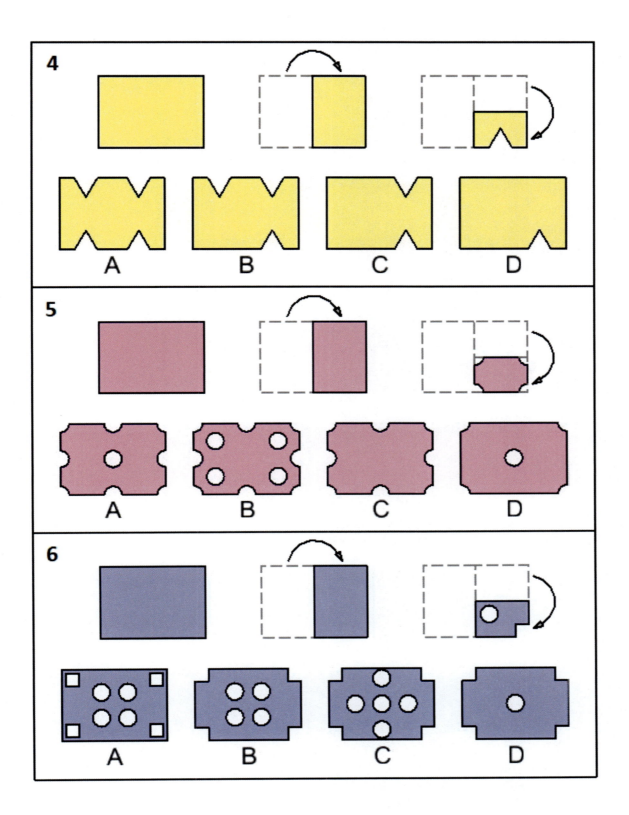

Answer Key

Matching Colors and Shapes

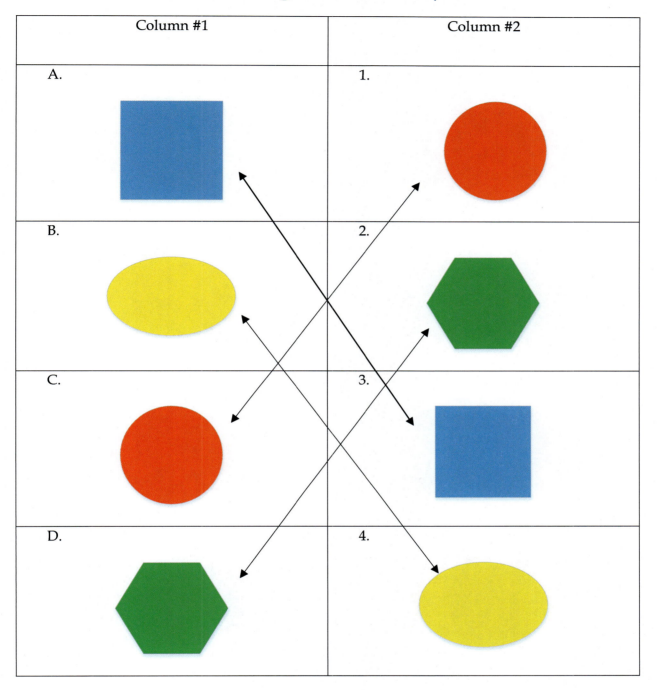

Matching only colors

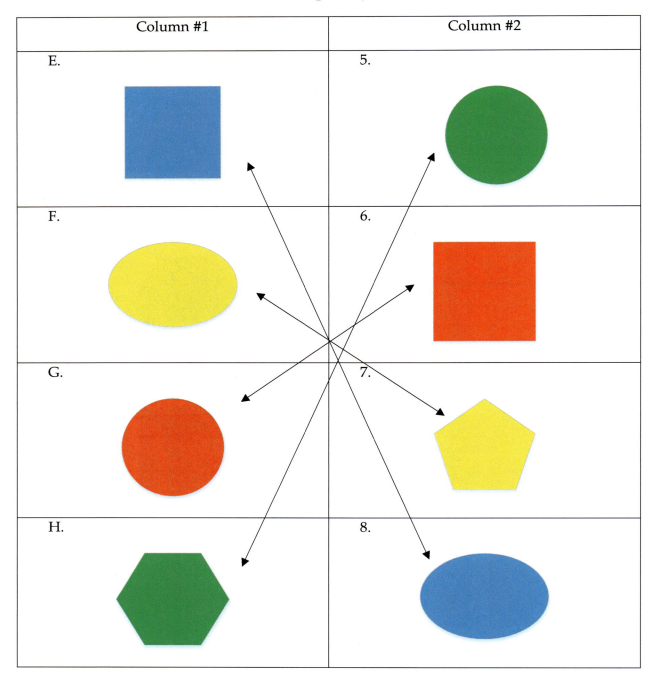

Matching Shading

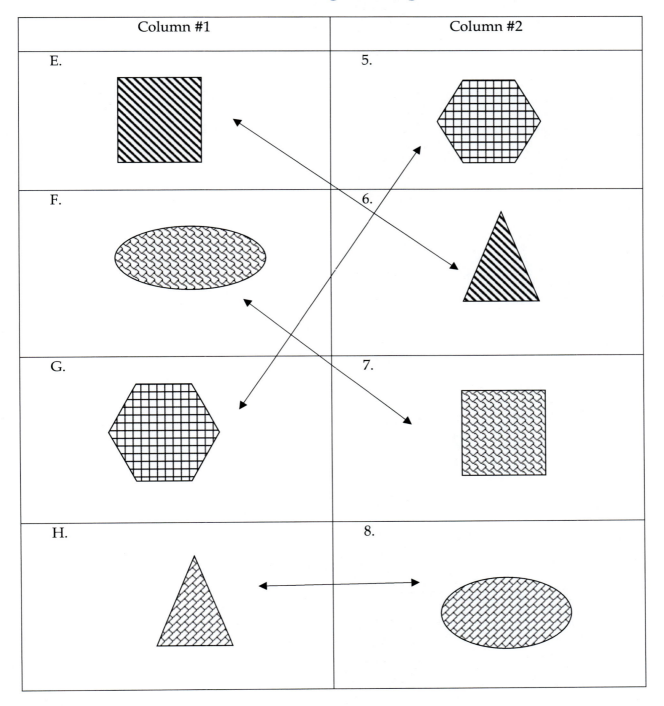

Number sequence

Complete the number sequence below by finding what number goes in place of the Question Mark (?)

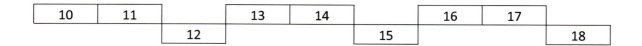

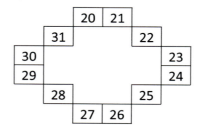

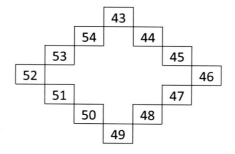

Deducing Numbers

Based on the following clues deduce and guess the number.

Clue #1: The number is between 1 and 10 ➔ this clue means number can be either 2, 3, 4, 5, 6, 7, 8 or 9
Clue #2: The number is greater than 5 ➔ this clue means number is either 6, 7, 8 or 9
Clue #3: The number is greater than 7 ➔ this clue means number is either 8 or 9
Clue #4: The number is less than 9 ➔ this clue means number is 8.

What is the number? 8

===

Clue #1: The number is a 2 digit number ➔ this clue means the number is either 10, 11 or some number less or equal to 99.
Clue #2: When you subtract 2 from this number, you get a one digit number ➔ this clue means that the number is either 10 or 11
Clue #3: The number is greater than 10 ➔ this clue means that the number is 11.

What is the number? 11

===

Clue #1: The number is between 1 and 20 ➔this clue means the number is either 2, 3 or some number less than 20.
Clue #2: The digit in the units place is 5 ➔this clue means that the number is either 5 or 15
Clue #3: The number is greater than 10 ➔ this clue means that the number is 15

What is the number? 15

===

Clue #1: The number is between 11 and 15 ➔this clue means the number is either 12, 13 or 14
Clue #2: The number is an even number ➔ this clue means the number is either 12 or 14
Clue #3: The number is closer to 15 than to 11 ➔ this clue means the number is 14

What is the number? 14

Connect Dots to form Shapes

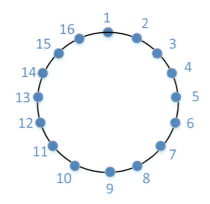
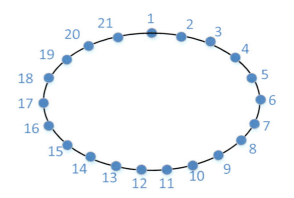
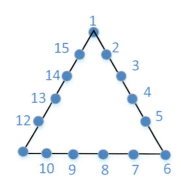
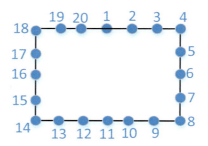
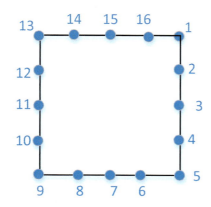
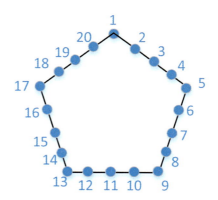

3 Sisters

Anna, Beth and Celeste are 3 sisters. With the following clues, can you guess who is the youngest one and the oldest of the 3 sisters?

Clue #1: Anna is not the youngest one.
Clue #2: Beth is not the oldest one.
Clue #3: Celeste is neither the oldest nor the youngest one.

	Youngest	Middle	Oldest
Clue #1		Anna	Anna
Clue #2	Beth	Beth	
Clue #3	Beth	Celeste	Anna

Confirmed order Beth is Youngest, Celeste is middle sibling and Anna is the oldest sister.

===

Anna, Beth and Celeste are into either water sport, biking or rugby. With the following clues, can you guess who plays what sport?

Clue #1: Anna doesn't like water sports.
Clue #2: Beth doesn't like biking cross country.
Clue #3: Celeste loves to play Rugby.

	Anna	Beth	Celeste
Clue #1		Water Sport	Water Sport
Clue #2	Biking		Biking
Clue #3			Rugby

Hence Anna likes biking, Beth enjoys water sports and Celeste plays rugby.

===

Anna, Beth and Celeste liked different cuisines. With the following clues, can you guess their favorite cuisine

Clue #1: Anna loves Italian Food
Clue #2: Beth doesn't like Greek Food but loves French Food
Clue #3: Celeste is opposite of Beth in terms of her favorite food.

	Anna	Beth	Celeste
Clue #1	Italian		
Clue #2		French	Greek
Clue #3			

Hence Anna likes Italian and Beth loves French cuisine, which leaves Celeste to like Greek food.

Matching Owls

Page 69

Matching Sizes

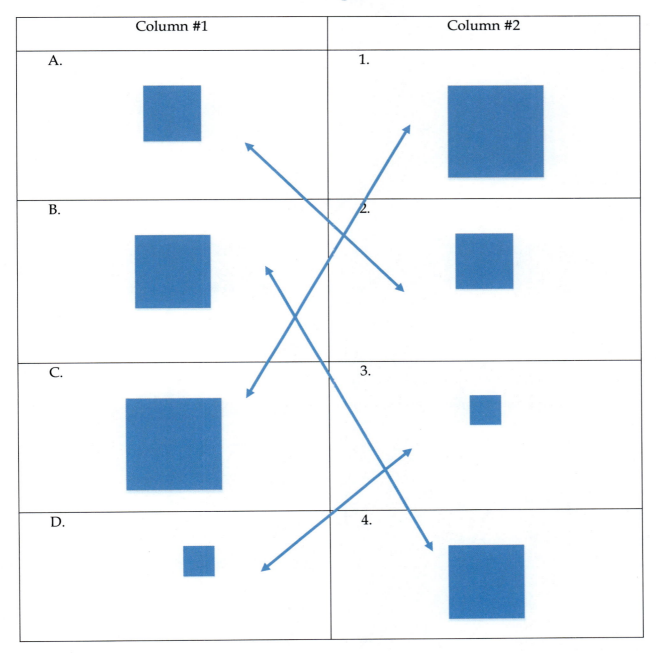

Matching Pair of Shapes

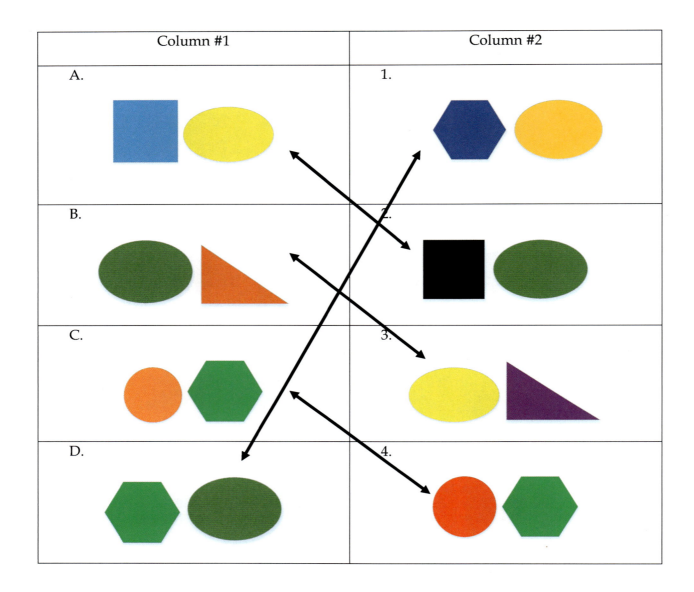

Describing Objects

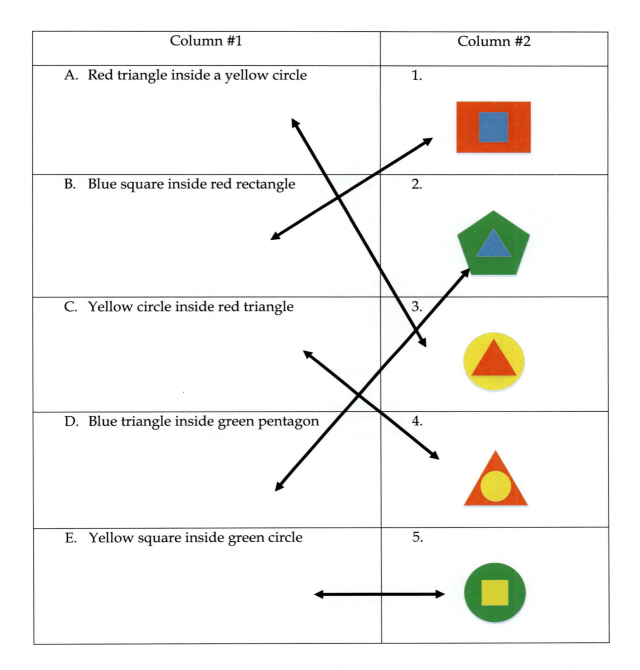

Matching Shadows

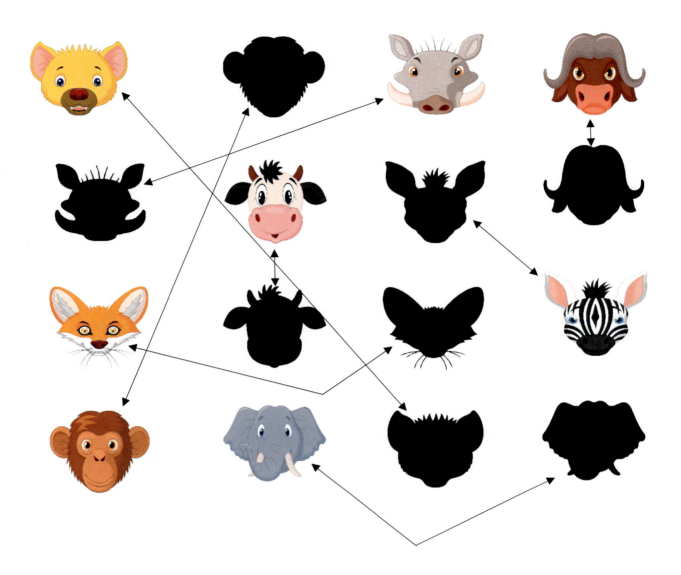

Finding Color Patterns

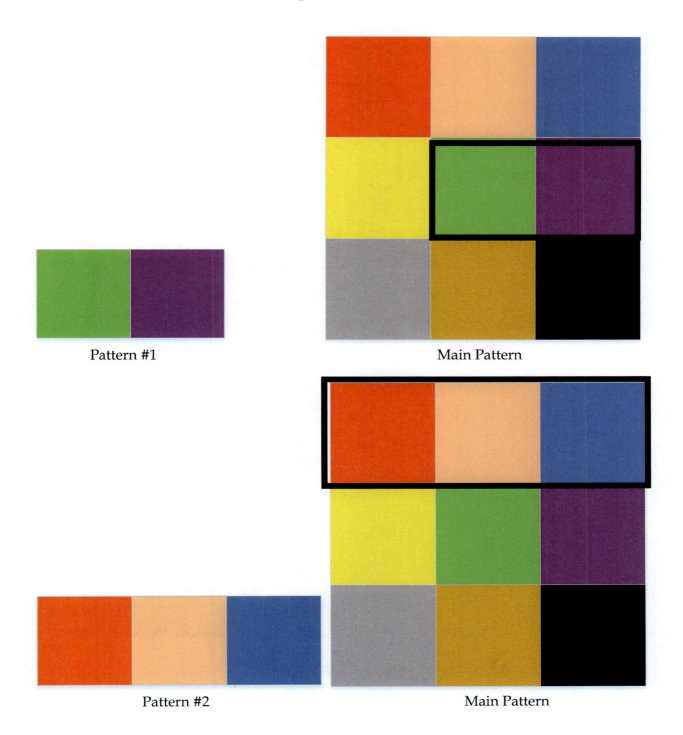

Pattern #1

Main Pattern

Pattern #2

Main Pattern

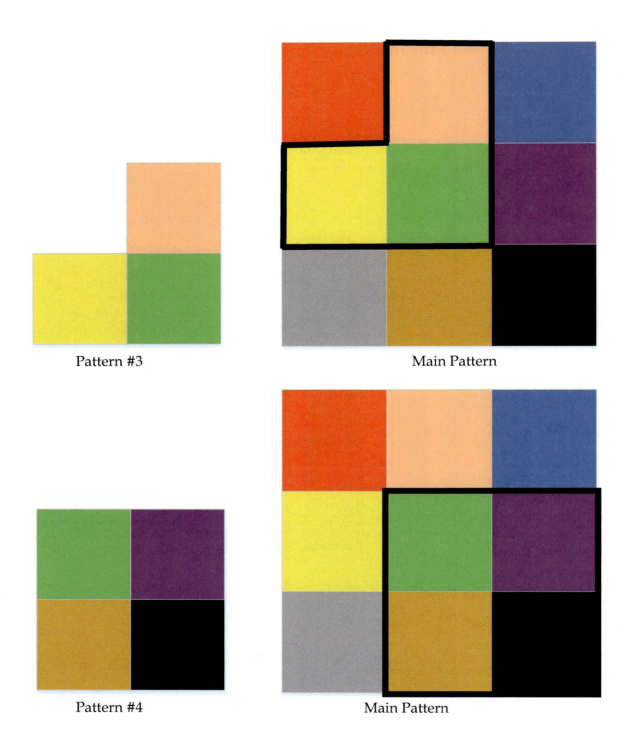

Pattern #3 Main Pattern

Pattern #4 Main Pattern

Match Stars

Column #1   Column #2

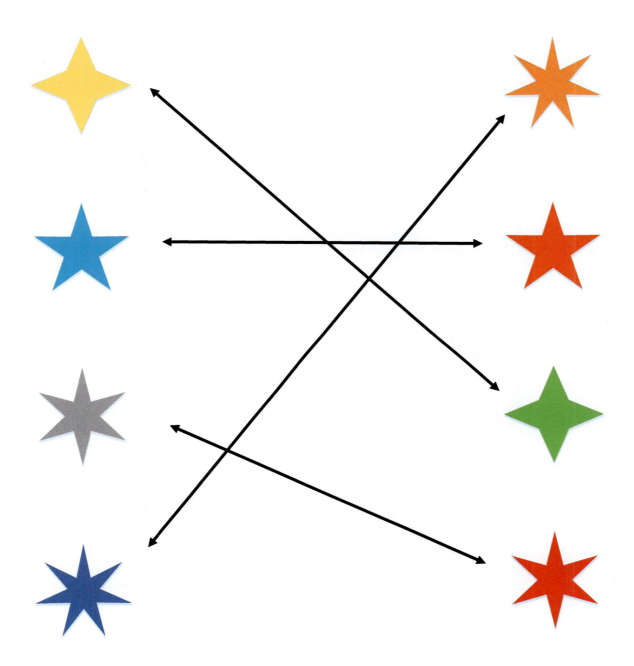

Overlapping Shapes

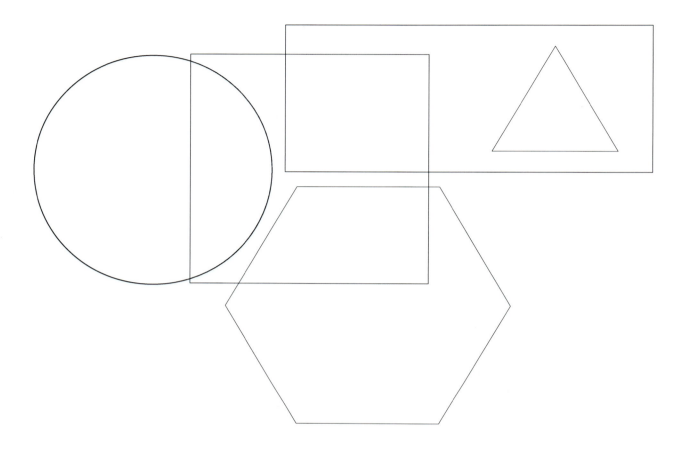

Does the Circle overlap with the Square?	Yes
Does the Square overlap with the Rectangle?	Yes
Does the Rectangle overlap with the Circle?	No
Does the Hexagon overlap with the Triangle?	No
Does the Circle overlap with the Triangle?	No
Does the Hexagon overlap with the Circle?	No

Similar Ladybugs

Shape Sequence

Circle the shape that should come next in the sequence of shapes given.

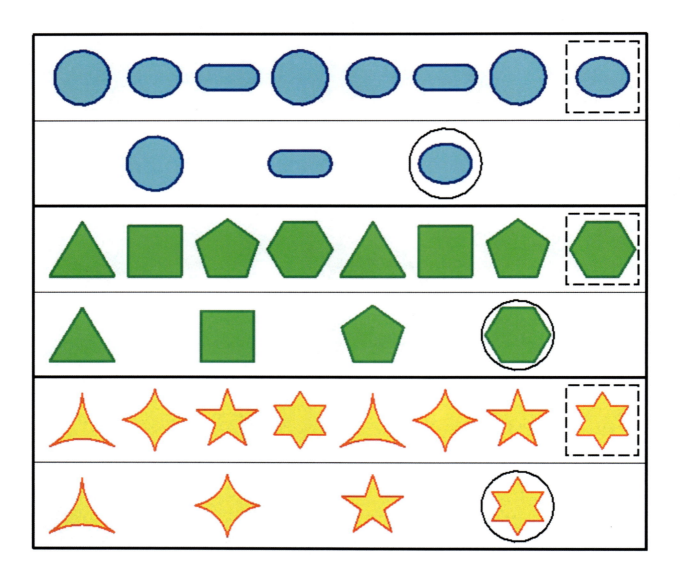

Number Sequence (Frog)

Where would the leaping frog land next?

The frog is leaping five paces each time

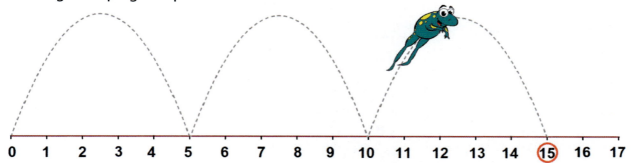

The frog is leaping four paces each time

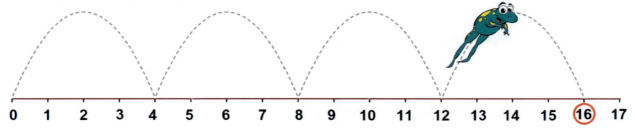

The frog is leaping three paces each time

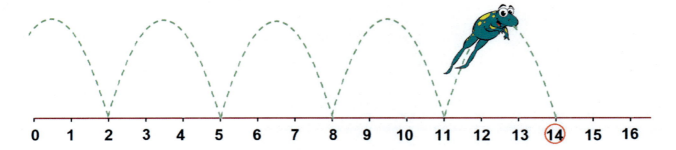

Number Sequence (Bouncing Ball)

Where would the ball land next?

The bouncing distance is reducing 4, 3, 2, 1

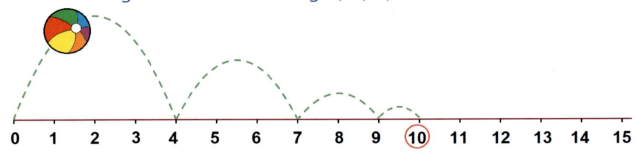

The bouncing distance is reducing 4, 3, 2, 1

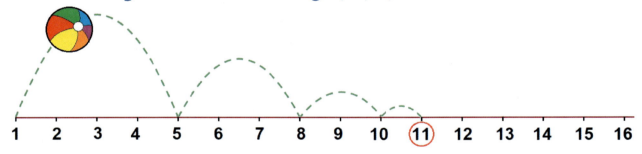

The bouncing distance is reducing 5, 4, 3, 2

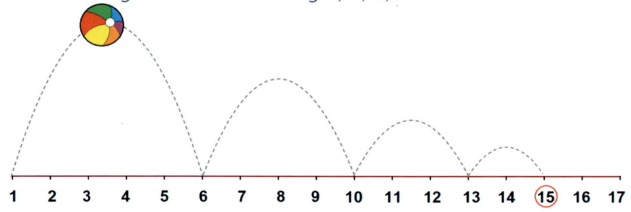

Alphabet Sequence

Which alphabet would come next in the sequence?

Alphabets **ABC** are repeating

A B C A B C A **B**

Alphabets **BBQ** are repeating

B B Q B B Q B B Q **B**

Alphabets **PQRS** are repeating

P Q R S P Q R S P **Q**

Alphabets **XYZZ** are repeating

X Y Z Z X Y Z Z X **Y**

Color Sequence

Which color would come next in the sequence?

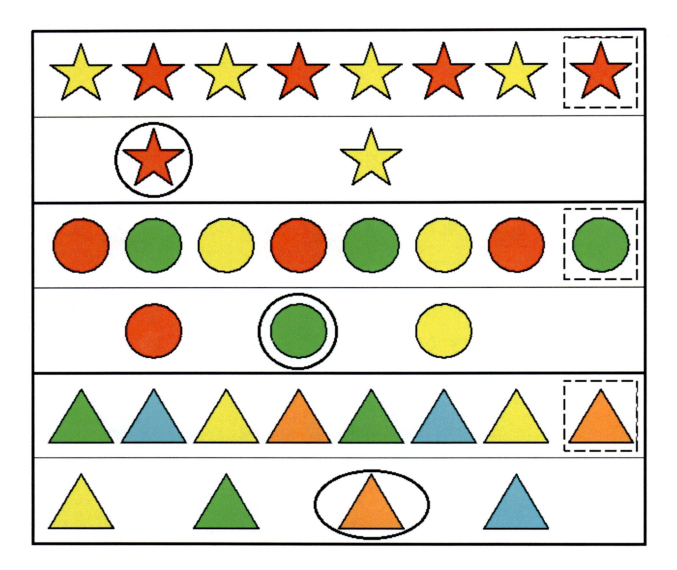

Missing Arrow

Box #1 and Box #2 both have various types of arrows. Find which arrow is present in Box #1 and missing from Box #2

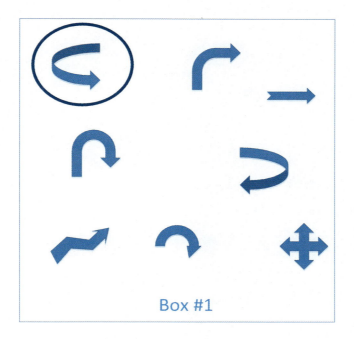

Box #1

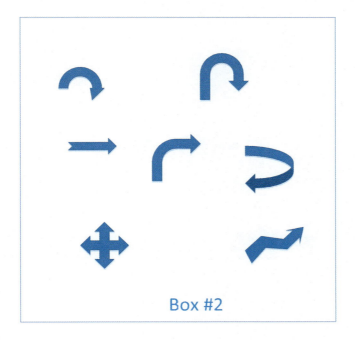

Box #2

Tangled Balloons

Page 85

Hidden Numbers #1

Hidden Numbers #2

Find Differences #1

Find Differences #2

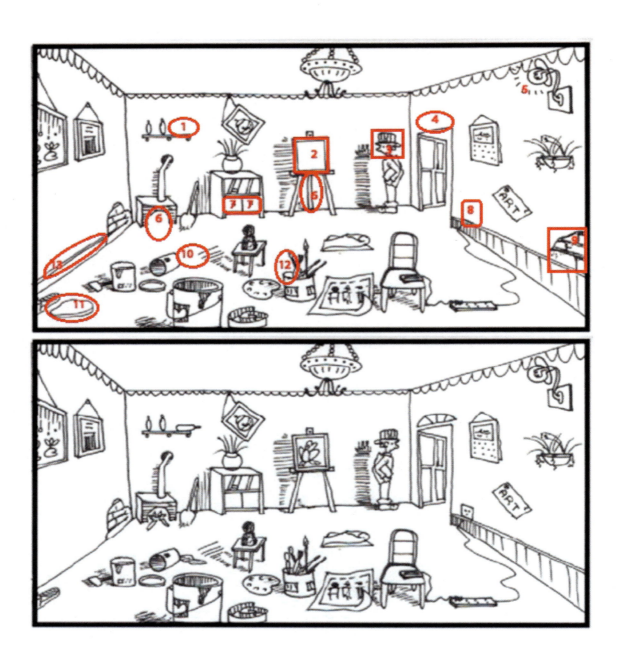

Find Differences #3

Find Differences #4

Find Differences #5

Math Match

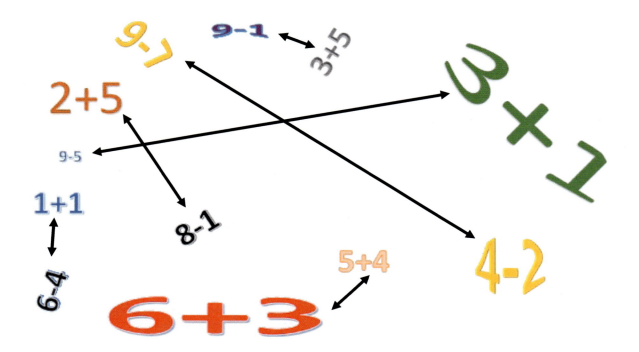

Animals in various shapes

Study the shapes and the position of the animals below. Answer questions below about how the animals are placed in the diagram

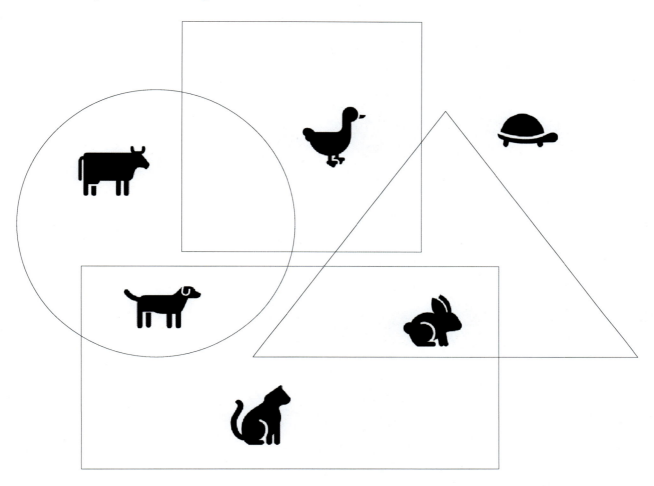

Which animal is inside the square?	Duck
Which animal is inside the circle as well as the rectangle?	Dog
Which animal or animals are inside the circle?	Cow and Dog
Which animal or animals are inside the rectangle?	Dog, Cat and Rabbit
Which animal or animals are not inside any of the shapes?	Turtle

Counting Shapes #1

Count the number of various shapes in the picture below

Counting Shapes #2

Page 96

Triangular Maze

Show the spaceship the path to the center of this triangular maze?

Matching Art Tiles

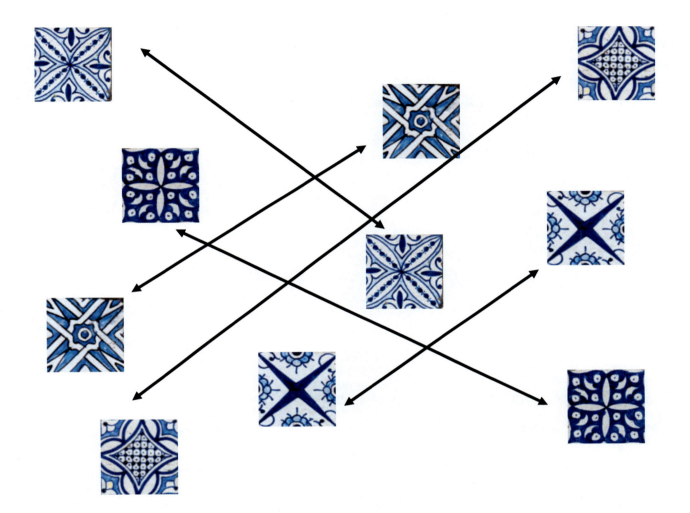

Find hidden Objects #1

Find hidden Objects #2

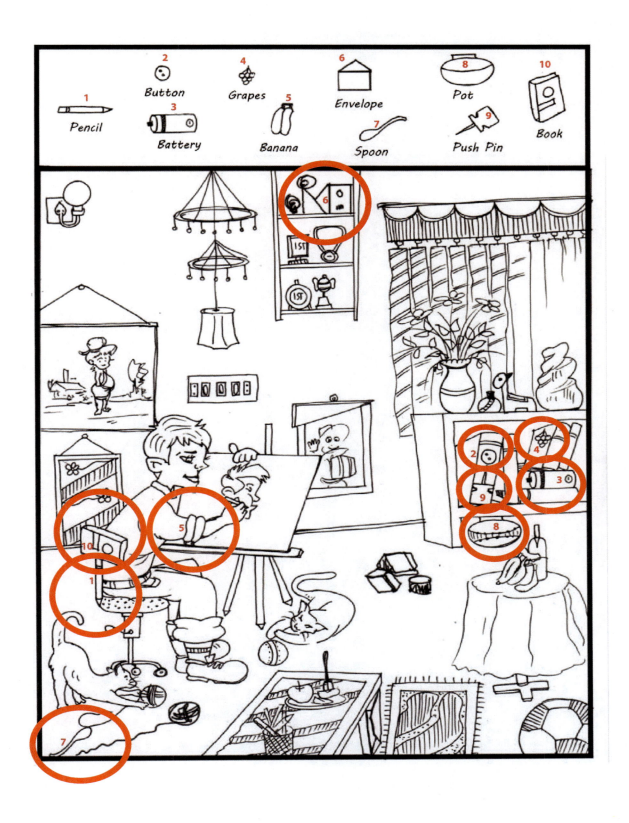

Find hidden Objects #3

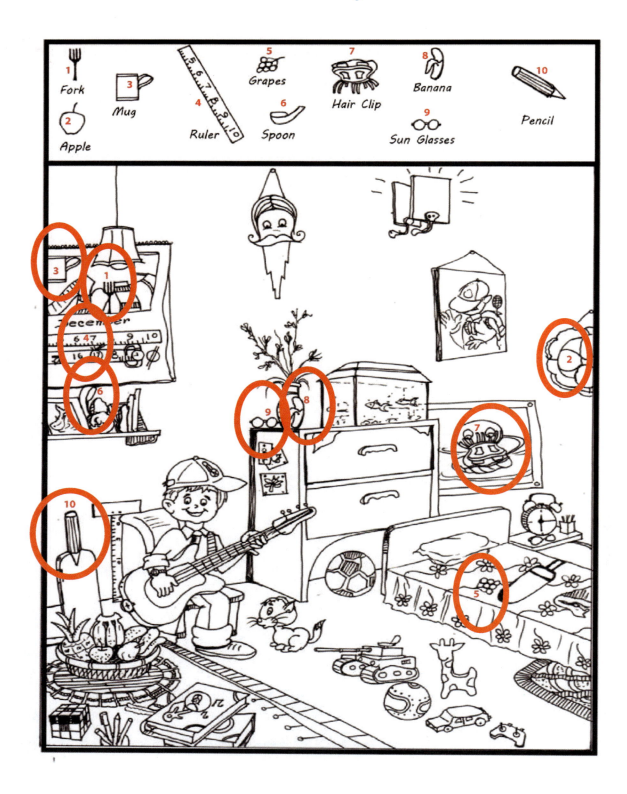

Find hidden Objects #4

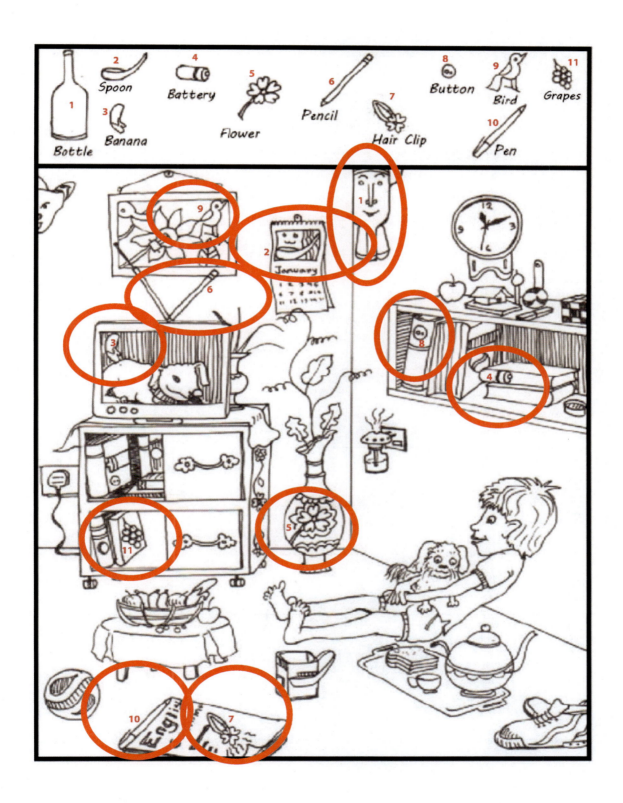

Find hidden Objects #5

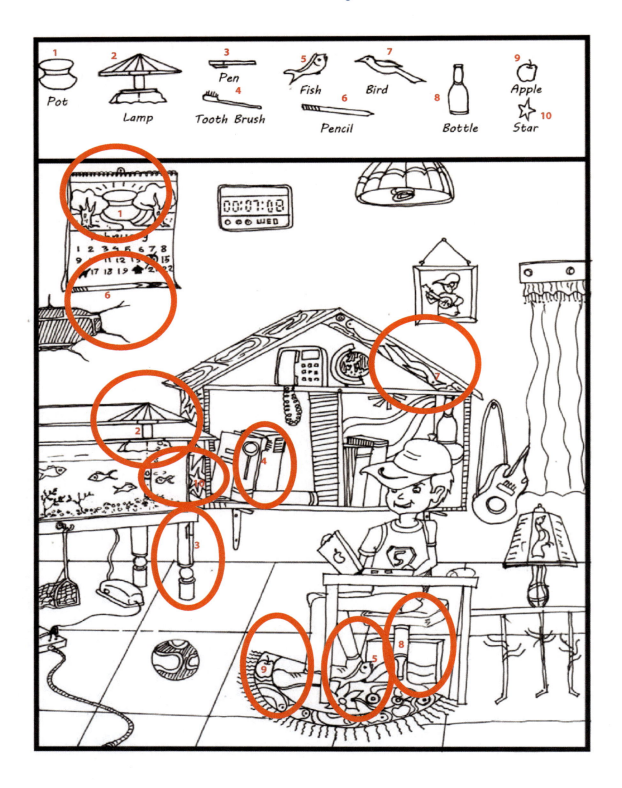

Ball and the Box

Select the word/words that describes the position of the ball

The ball is (**in front of**) the box	The ball is (**behind**) the box
The ball is (**inside**) the box	The ball is (**outside**) the box
The ball is (**under**) the box	The ball is (**on**) the box
The ball is (**below**) the box	The ball is (**above**) the box
The ball is on the (**right**) of the box	The ball is on the (**left**) of the box

Identifying Objects

1. Which of the following would you wear to protect your head from the cold?

A

2. Which of the following would you use to protect your eyes from the sunlight?

A

3. Which of the following has a hard and thorny skin?

D

Puzzling Family

1. Jessica Johnson has a younger brother Alex Johnson. Alex is taller than Jessica. Jessica's mother Alicia is taller than Alex. Which picture below would be the right picture for the family?

A

2. Victoria got into trouble and was given a timeout and asked to spend the day in her room. She was not allowed to play with her video games or dolls or watch TV. Which is the one object she can use in her room during her timeout?

C

3. Mary's younger brother is 6 years old. Her older brother is 9 years old. How old can Mary be?

7

C

Bug Search

1. See the picture of the bug inside the box. Search for the same bug in the group of bugs marked #1 to #5.

                                              #1   #2   #3   #4   #5

2. See the picture of the bug inside the box. Search for the same bug in the group of bugs marked #1 to #5.

                                              #1   #2   #3   #4   #5

3. See the picture of the bug inside the box. Search for the same bug in the group of bugs marked #1 to #5.

                                              #1   #2   #3   #4   #5

Paper Folding

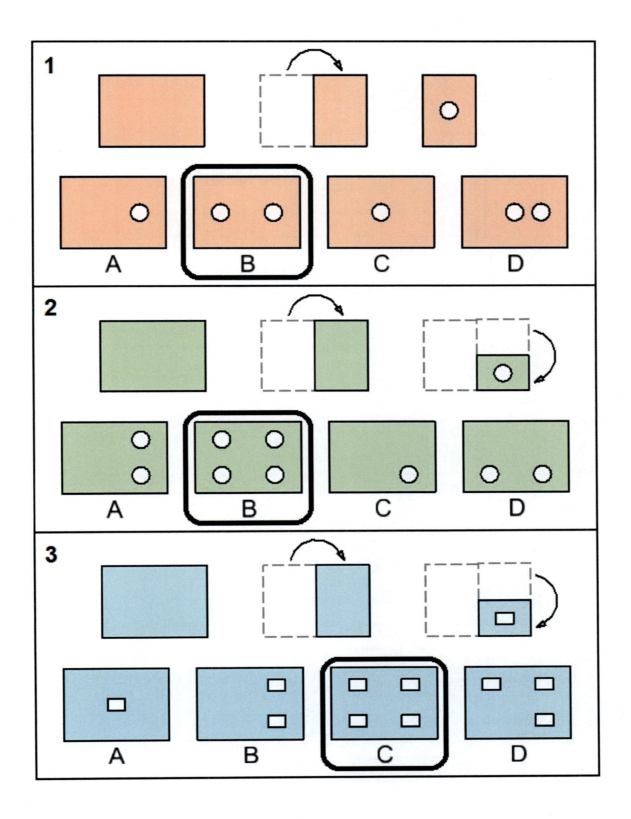

Paper Folding

Made in the USA
Coppell, TX
30 April 2021